THIS JOURNAL BELONGS TO:

_____

DAD

&

_____

Daughter

Copyright © 2021 by Danielle Fairbairn-Bland

All rights reserved.

No part of this publication may be reproduced, distributed, or transmitted in any form or by any means, including photocopying, recording, or other electronic or mechanical methods, without the prior written permission of the publisher, except in the case of brief quotations embodied in critical reviews and certain other noncommercial uses permitted by copyright law.

Made 2 Heal
New York, NY
ISBN: 978-1-7367094-0-5

For more journals, visit us online at www.deefbland.com or email info@deefbland.com

This book is dedicated to fathers and father figures that protect, love and support their daughters unconditionally. You are powerful, worthy and necessary!

Signed,
Daddy's Girl

How to use this book

Journal at your own pace.
There is no right or wrong way to journal. Take your time and figure out what works best for the both of you.

Have an open mind and listen with your heart.
Be open to the experience and listen without judgement.

Make it work for the both of you.
This experience is all about the both of you! Discuss your expectations and what you hope to gain from each other.

Establish rules for privacy.
Discuss the expectations for sharing with others. Can others read the journal? Can you discuss what is shared with others?

Go beyond these pages
This is just the beginning-continue to build and connect outside of these pages.

When I first held you in my arms...

Daughter

My first memory of us...

DAD

Having you as my daughter...

Daughter

Having you as my dad...

Dear DAD,

Love,

NOTE TO SELF

I remember when...

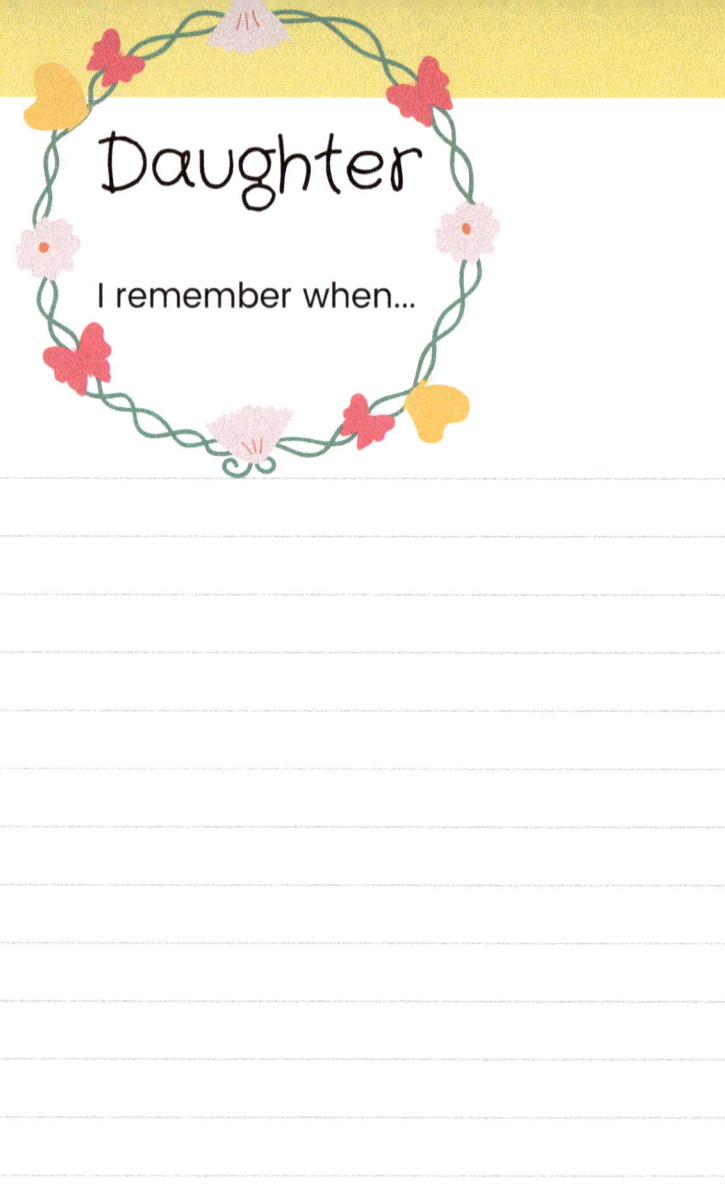

Daughter

I remember when...

DAD & Daughter

What does this mean to you both?

JOY

FORGIVENESS

DAD

You've helped me to...

Daughter

You've helped me to...

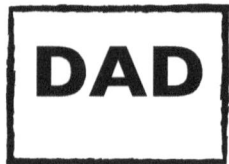

Watching you grow up, my favorite memory so far is...

Daughter

Growing up, my favorite memory was...

Dance Break

TAKE A MOMENT TO BREATHE.

BREATHE IN...

BREATHE OUT...

BREATHE IN...

BREATHE OUT.

Growing up, my favorite food was...

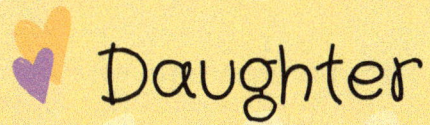 Daughter

Growing up, my favorite food was...

NOTE TO SELF

NOTE TO SELF

Dear Daughter,

Love,

OUR MEMORIES

DAD

Daughter

PHOTO HERE

PHOTO HERE

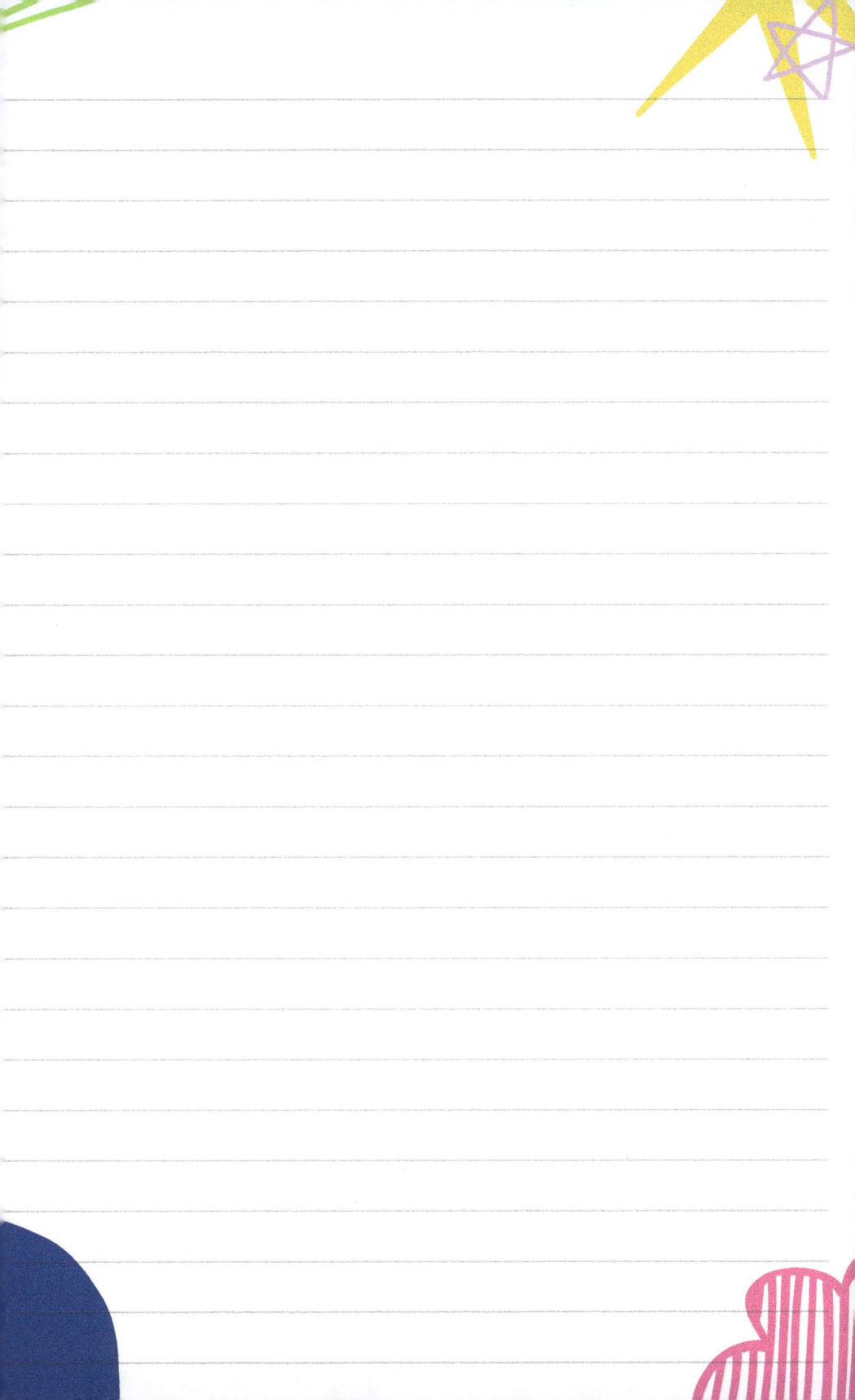

OUR RELATIONSHIP

6 words to describe our relationship.

OUR RELATIONSHIP

STRENGTHS OF OUR RELATIONSHIP.

AREAS OF IMPROVEMENT.

OUR RELATIONSHIP

OUR RELATIONSHIP

Here & Now

DAD

When I look at you, I am amazed at how:

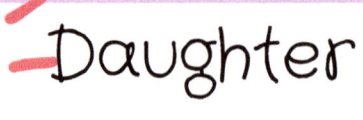 # Daughter

When I look at you, I am amazed at how:

DAD

If I could travel anywhere right now, I would travel to

Daughter

If I could travel anywhere right now, I would travel to

DAD

MY BUCKET LIST

DAD

Describe your daughter in 5 words.

Daughter

Describe your dad in 5 words.

I am passionate about...

Daughter

I am passionate about...

The most difficult time in my life...

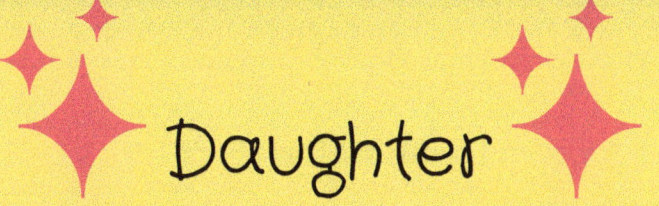

Daughter

The most difficult time in my life...

ASK ME ANYTHING

MOMENT OF GRATITUDE

DAD

DAUGHTER

Dear Daughter,

Love,

Let's talk about Identity
(I can only be ME)

What do you want to share with your daughter?

What do you want to share with your dad?

WHAT DO YOU BOTH WANT TO LEARN MORE ABOUT?

Let's talk about Relationships
(We are better together)

What do you want to share with your daughter?

What do you want to share with your dad?

WHAT DO YOU BOTH WANT TO LEARN MORE ABOUT?

TAKE A MOMENT TO BREATHE.

BREATHE IN...

BREATHE OUT...

BREATHE IN...

BREATHE OUT.

Let's talk about Self Esteem
(Flaws & All)

What do you want to share with your daughter?

What do you want to share with your dad?

WHAT DO YOU BOTH WANT TO LEARN MORE ABOUT?

Let's talk about Personal Development
(Goals | Purpose | Passion)

What do you want to share with your daughter?

What do you want to share with your dad?

WHAT DO YOU BOTH WANT TO LEARN MORE ABOUT?

Let's talk about Finances
(Saving | Investing | Spending | Income)

What do you want to share with your daughter?

What do you want to share with your dad?

WHAT DO YOU BOTH WANT TO LEARN MORE ABOUT?

Let's talk about Health
(Investing in your mind, body and soul)

What do you want to share with your daughter?

What do you want to share with your dad?

WHAT DO YOU BOTH WANT TO LEARN MORE ABOUT?

Let's talk about Mental Wellness
(Inhale, Exhale, Repeat)

What do you want to share with your daughter?

What do you want to share with your dad?

WHAT DO YOU BOTH WANT TO LEARN MORE ABOUT?

Reflections

What did you enjoy about journaling?

What did you learn?

I want to learn more about…

www.ingramcontent.com/pod-product-compliance
Lightning Source LLC
Chambersburg PA
CBHW040108120526
44589CB00040B/2823